P9-DCV-095

Weather

Lisa M. Gerry

NATIONAL
GEOGRAPHIC
KiDS

WASHINGTON, D.C.

Whoosh!

The wind blows through the trees, and the long branches sway and dance in the breeze. It's a windy day.

Windy, sunny, and rainy are all different kinds of weather. Weather is always changing. Just watch, you'll see!

The wind can be fast or slow. It can push boats across water and blow hats off heads.

Whoops!

Sunshine!

On sunny days, the sun shines bright, warming the earth.

Sunflowers and daisies turn toward the sun to soak up as many of its rays as they can.

The sun can
make the air
feel hot, just right for
a rest in the shade ...

Clouds!

Clouds are made of tiny drops of water that float together in the sky.

Fluffy white clouds are cumulus clouds. Can you say KYOOM-yuh-lus?

On sunny days, you might see big puffy clouds. When they block the sun, they make patches of shade on the ground below.

Some clouds are thin and feathery and float high in the sky.

Thin and wispy clouds are called cirrus clouds. Can you say SEER-us?

Flat gray clouds are called stratus clouds. Can you say STRA-tus?

Some clouds cover the sky like thick gray blankets.

15

Plants and animals need rain to survive.

Drip, drop!

When dark clouds roll in, rain might be next. One by one, drops of water fall from the clouds above.

Pitter-patter, split-splat.

Brrr!

When it's cold enough,
water droplets in the clouds
can freeze and fall
to the ground
as snow.

18

Down drift snowflakes,
one by one.

19

Thunder
always comes
after lightning.

20

When thunder rumbles and lightning flashes through the sky, get ready for a thunderstorm.

Thunderstorms can bring lots of rain and lots of loud noise.

Boom!

After a storm ends,
the sun peeks
through the clouds
again. Animals
shake the
rain off.

Let's go outside! The sun is shining. There are puddles to splash in ...

Wow!

... and rainbows to see.

24

A rainbow happens when sunlight shines through tiny raindrops floating in the air.

Have you ever seen a rainbow?

25

Wild Weather

Here are some ways
that weather
can be wild.

FLOOD
When too much
rain falls too fast, it
can cause floods.

TORNADO
When very strong
winds start
spinning, they can
form a tornado.

HURRICANE
A hurricane is a widespread storm that brings strong winds and heavy rain.

BLIZZARD
A blizzard is a heavy snowstorm with strong winds.

HAIL
Balls of ice called hail sometimes rain down from the sky.

DROUGHT
A drought happens when it doesn't rain for a very long time. It can make the ground dry up and crack.

27

Which kind of weather do you like best? Why?

Watching the Weather

Scientists who study the weather are called meteorologists. Here are some of the tools they use to predict what the weather will be like.

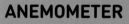

ANEMOMETER
An anemometer measures wind speed.

SATELLITE
A satellite in space takes pictures that show scientists how clouds are moving across Earth.

THERMOMETER
A thermometer measures air temperature—how warm or cold it is.

WEATHER BALLOON
A weather balloon goes up high in the sky. It sends scientists information about the conditions up there.

What is today's weather like where you live?

WINDSOCK
A windsock shows which way the wind is blowing.

RAIN GAUGE
A rain gauge measures how much rain has fallen.

What Should You Wear?

When you head outside, it's important to have the right gear for the day's weather. Can you match these clothes and other items with the weather they are best for?

SUNNY & HOT

RAINY & WET

SNOWY & COLD

For Abby, Andy, and Jackson, with whom it's always sunny—L.M.G.

Copyright © 2018 National Geographic Partners, LLC

Published by National Geographic Partners, LLC. All rights reserved. Reproduction of the whole or any part of the contents without written permission from the publisher is prohibited.

Since 1888, the National Geographic Society has funded more than 12,000 research, exploration, and preservation projects around the world. The Society receives funds from National Geographic Partners, LLC, funded in part by your purchase. A portion of the proceeds from this book supports this vital work. To learn more, visit natgeo.com/info.

NATIONAL GEOGRAPHIC and Yellow Border Design are trademarks of the National Geographic Society, used under license.

Library of Congress Cataloging-in-Publication Data

Names: Gerry, Lisa, author. | National Geographic Society (U.S.), publisher.
Title: Explore my world : weather / By Lisa M. Gerry.
Other titles: National Geographic kids.
Description: Washington, DC : National Geographic Kids, [2018] | Series: Explore my world | Audience: Ages 3-7. | Audience: K to Grade 3.
Identifiers: LCCN 2017050020 (print) | LCCN 2017060677 (ebook) | ISBN 9781426332609 (ebook) | ISBN 9781426331558 (pbk.) | ISBN 9781426331565 (hardcover)
Subjects: LCSH: Weather--Juvenile literature. | Weather--Miscellanea--Juvenile literature. | CYAC: Weather. | LCGFT: Picture books. | Illustrated works.
Classification: LCC QC981.3 (ebook) | LCC QC981.3 .G47 2018 (print) | DDC 551.6--dc23
LC record available at https://lccn.loc.gov/2017050020

Designed by Sanjida Rashid

The publisher gratefully acknowledges meteorologist Nicolas Lopez for his expert review of this book.

Printed in China
18/RRDS/1

Animal names by page number:
Cover: chinstrap penguin
Page 1: red-eyed tree frog
Pages 2–3: Siberian tiger
Page 6: red fox
Page 10: white-tailed deer
Page 11: Alaskan brown bear
Page 15: giraffe
Page 16: assassin bug (on flower) and leopard gecko
Page 17: blue tit
Page 18: red squirrel
Page 19: gray wolves
Page 21: African elephants
Page 22: African lion

ILLUSTRATIONS CREDITS
Front cover: Mihai Simonia/Shutterstock; (CTR RT), Ira Meyer/National Geographic Creative; (LO RT), Mimadeo/Shutterstock; **Back cover:** Kurt Kleemann/Shutterstock; 1, Michael Durham/Minden Pictures; 2-3, Ondrej Prosicky/Shutterstock; 4-5, Andriy Blokhin/Shutterstock; 6 (LE), Sumroeng Chinnapan/Shutterstock; 6 (RT), AngelaLouwe/Shutterstock; 7, Jochem D Wijnands/Getty Images; 8, OHishiapply/Shutterstock; 9, Bayanova Svetlana/Shutterstock; 10, Photology1971/Getty Images; 11, EEI_Tony/Getty Images; 12, Slavko Sereda/Shutterstock; 13 (LE), Korionov/Shutterstock; 13 (RT), Janis Smits/Shutterstock; 14 (UP), Roblan/Shutterstock; 14 (LO), CE Photography/Shutterstock; 15, Utopia_88/Getty Images; 16, shikheigoh/Getty Images; 17 (UP), Mr Twister/Shutterstock; 17 (LO), Menno Schaefer/Shutterstock; 18 (UP), Ariel Skelley/Getty Images; 18 (LO), Giedriius/Shutterstock; 19, rogertrentham/Getty Images; 20, Mihai Simonia/Shutterstock; 21, Denis-Huot/Nature Picture Library; 22 (UP), Mr. Wichai Thongtape/Shutterstock; 22 (LO), Denis-Huot/Nature Picture Library; 23, real444/Getty Images; 24-25, valio84sl/Getty Images; 26 (LE), Minerva Studio/Shutterstock; 26 (RT), Jaroslav Moravcik/Shutterstock; 27 (UP LE), RamonBerk/Getty Images; 27 (UP RT), Evannovostro/Shutterstock; 27 (LO LE), Mykola Mazuryk/Shutterstock; 27 (LO RT), swkunst/Getty Images; 28 (LE), Andrey Armyagov/Shutterstock; 28 (RT), Natthawon Chaosakun/Shutterstock; 29 (UP LE), Paul Nicklen/National Geographic Creative; 29 (UP RT), T.W. van Urk/Shutterstock; 29 (LO LE), Labrador Photo Video/Shutterstock; 29 (LO RT), BMJ/Shutterstock; 30 (UP), Smileus/Dreamstime; 30 (CTR), peresanz/Shutterstock; 30 (LO), Andrew Mayovskyy/Shutterstock; 31 (UP LE), Khongkitwiriyachan/Dreamstime; 31 (UP CTR), Sarycheva Olesia/Shutterstock; 31 (UP RT), Olesia Bilkei/Shutterstock; 31 (CTR LE), cookelma/Getty Images; 31 (CTR CTR), tale/Shutterstock; 31 (CTR RT), sagir/Shutterstock; 31 (LO LE), BW Folsom/Shutterstock; 31 (LO CTR), Serhii Tsyhanok/Shutterstock; 31 (LO RT), photoDISC; 32, yevgeniy11/Shutterstock